GLEANINGS

Fragments of Life Experiences

Poems

by
Sister M. Rita Prendergast, C.C.V.I.

Gleaning was a common practice in ancient Israel. It was a form of charity for the disadvantaged in society. (See Leviticus 23:22 and Deuteronomy 24:19.) Groups of the poor, such as widows, orphans and foreigners, could walk behind the harvesters, picking up what was left to feed the hungry. The title <u>Gleanings</u> was inspired by Jean François Millet painting "The Gleaners", that depicts this practice.

ISBN 978-0-692-48624-5

Printed in the United States of America
Litho Press Inc.

Table of Contents

1970's

1980's

1990's

2000's

Foreword

Growing up in County Kildare, Ireland, Sister Rita Prendergast probably never envisioned that her life would take so many interesting turns, beginning with her entrance into a congregation of religious sisters in Texas and becoming involved in the teaching ministry of the Sisters of Charity of the Incarnate Word. In preparation for her ministry, she became a student at Incarnate Word College in San Antonio, where, she maintains, her love of both reading and writing poetry began. She continued her education at The Catholic University of America in Washington, D.C., earned both a Bachelor's and a Master's degree in English, and was elected to the national honor society, Phi Beta Kappa. Upon the completion of her degrees, she returned to San Antonio and spent several years as Assistant Professor of English at Incarnate Word College.

She later earned the Higher Diploma/Education at the National University of Ireland and was responsible for the establishment of a new secondary school (also called Incarnate Word College) in Dunmore, County Galway. Sister Rita was the founder, the first principal, and instructor in English.

After several years in this position, she returned to the United States, where her love of literature and language led her to other areas of study, including the teaching of English as a foreign language. She earned a certificate in this area of study at Georgetown University and began her work at Lackland Air Force Base's Defense Language Institute working with air force recruits. She later applied her skills in working with students in foreign countries where she served as a missionary, including Mexico, Peru, and Africa. At the same time, she expanded her own knowledge and use of the languages of these countries and combined her teaching and writing with the work of translation.

Sensitivity to the spoken and written word is present in all of Sister Rita's poetry. She shows a fascination with words and phrases, questioning their meanings, wondering about their popular and proper usage. She seems also to exaggerate the forceful parts of the language, even to the point of eliminating the prepositions, articles, and conjunctions, the weaker parts of expression that sometimes get in the way. Punctuation also seems to be unnecessary and only a distraction from the meaning.

In addition to her love of language, Sister Rita's poetry reflects her love of God and God's people. Over and over again, she looks into her own heart and mind and challenges her reader to do likewise to encounter the all-loving and all-merciful Creator. Getting to the heart of the matter is what seems to matter most. Say what you mean and mean what you say, distinguishing the genuine and the true from what is false and artificial. Finally, throughout it all, Sister Rita has a great sense of humor that breaks through at unexpected times, taking the reader by surprise and challenging others, as she does herself, to put all things into perspective.

Sister Margaret Patrice Slattery, Ph.D.
President Emerita Incarnate Word College

Introduction

My book is entitled *Gleanings* because my poems were written (gleaned) throughout my working life. There was no sabbatical in a quiet cottage on Cape Cod with somebody serving my meals while I dreamily waited for inspiration from earth, sky, and sea. I wrote or started poems "in between," jotting down a word, a line, an idea that called for more. This could happen anywhere any time: on a bus, looking down on snow patches on my way to my brother's home in New Jersey, doodling at a meeting, re-reading Emily Dickinson, or learning the year was Jonathan Swift's 500th anniversary. Some poems simply died at their genesis. I either lost the notes or just did not get back to them.

Another reason for the title of *Gleanings*, I simply like the word. I like the biblical connection with the story of Naomi and Ruth, two widows, mother-in-law and daughter-in-law, poor and needy, finding help from a rich and generous landowner who allowed them to glean his wheat fields after harvesting, instructing his workers to drop sheaves along the way for the gleaners. Growing up I was familiar with a painting of three women gleaners in biblical times which I later learned included Naomi and Ruth. That is the painting on the cover of this book, a work completed in 1857 by Jean François Millet, entitled "The Gleaners" *(Des Glaneuses)*.

I wrote my first poem as an assignment in English 101 at Incarnate Word College, now University of the Incarnate Word. In grade and high school in Ireland we had memorized poems on which we were examined daily in class and later in state examinations. However, emphasis in English was on writing essays and compositions, also examined by the state. There was no writing of poetry. I don't remember ever being taught how to write a poem. Over time I was gradually introduced to poetic lore from the couplet and the sonnet to blank verse and free verse. When I discovered Roget's Thesaurus, I became excited and fascinated with the search for the exact word, wanting to have "the best words used in the best order" in all my poems.

As a Sister of Charity of the Incarnate Word I went from San Antonio in 1963 to serve as Principal of a new high school opened in Dunmore, Co. Galway. The Incarnate Word Sisters had established a vocation center there for the recruitment and preparation of young women to join in the Congregation's Texas mission. In 1966, Ireland celebrated the 1916 rebellion achieving Irish freedom from British rule for which we had long yearned and fought for. The new government proclaimed "the Irish Republic as a Sovereign Independent State." This fiftieth anniversary celebration of Irish freedom, after some 800 years of colonization and slavery, included competitions in all the arts, open to Irish people wherever they might be. There was a section for schools, all levels. When my poem "Perspective: 1916-1966" won the prize for English poetry, I was more shocked than amazed and was encouraged in my efforts at poetry. After all, it was the first time one of my poems was judged by professionals and it was not found wanting. So now I joyfully keep on gleaning.

Sister M. Rita Prendergast, C.C.V.I.
B.A, M.A., Catholic University of America, Washington, D.C.
Higher Diploma in Education, Nat'l. University of Ireland

Dedication

My God

My Family

The Presentation Sisters, Kildare Town, Ireland

The Sisters of Charity of the Incarnate Word

A Hopeful Sigh

Oh would that I were what I'm meant to be

In faith and hope strong, filled with charity

And would that I had reached the appointed goal

Which God has set for my immortal soul.

Then fearless would I face the thief of night

Who comes to separate, as is His right,

Body and soul in parting that will last

Until the trumpet sounds with piercing blast,

Summoning sheep and goats in final meet

To stand before that awful judgment seat.

Yes, unafraid before Thee would I stand

Had I fulfilled, dear Lord, Thy least command.

Yet even now with Dismas, I dare plead

"Remember me" when you allot the Mead.

Emmanuel Triptych

I

AVE, EVA

There was a woman
Born of woman
Who was Mother to One born of God
In any man's cave, long, long ago
At lowly Bethlehem.

There was a woman
Formed of man
By God
Who – helped
Brought desolation
To the world called home.

She was the seed for us all,
For the woman born of woman
Who Mothered the One
Born of God
In any man's cave, long long ago
At lowly Bethlehem.

II

Paradox

Old as eternity

Young as tomorrow

Daystar in darkness

Night in the sun

Bread to the body

Hunger to soul

Lover of One

Lover of all

Changing to change us

And yet ever changeless

Death in all life

And birth in all death

This Phoenix, He came

And is coming yet

From night-womb

Day-lighted

And shouting

That's silent

To sear us and save us   Forever.

III

Response to e.e's coming

All Right God.

i'm coming   too

so   StopYourshoutingnow.   my ears

are Tired.   i've

learned the lesson: i'll give

the LOAF

or TWO.

NO!   all i've got.

H E R E   !

francis thompson was   (all) Right.

4

Wrestling

I lay in mire and mud defiled, degraded

And closed my ears to fumblings of your grace

While further, deeper, downwards in the pit

Of filth and filth and filth I ever wallowed

Not smelling, hearing, seeing, tasting, touching

The untired being of your eternal pursuit

But Godness never tires of the pursuit

And so you caught me, flagging foul forgotten

Resting, rationally, reasoning on my reins

And with divine finesse halted my endeavors

To find the fallow that would match my frame

Thus did you draw me through divinest unction

Of sacerdotal words that healed my wounds

Unto paths permitting not room but peace.

Fragment

Why blame the two who first said "No."
When there're Adams and Eves
Wherever you go.
And we all have a Macbeth hand in sleeve
That none but God Himself can relieve.

Palm Tree in the Cement

Why must you grow up in the arid ground
By fruitless earth encased and hemmed all 'round?
Does your still growing strength the lifeless cement
Of Man's making outpush and from the inside dent?
How come you can ensure that you have space
Your darkened tentacles beneath the road to trace?
Is it you, oh tall straight tree of fernlike head
With long grass leaves that by the wind are spread?
Is it you, just you that sends down under root
And trunk and leaves of beauty high upshoot?
Or is there something, someone else outside you
That causes you to grow and breathe as I do?
Answer me oh climbing Texas palm and tell
"It's Him Whom I have honored and dishonored well."

Fiat[1]

I left them to cross a wide, wide ocean
I left them to find a better good
I left them, all empty of emotion
I left them for things not understood
I left them that I might love them more
I left them not knowing then that when
I left them, love to heights unknown could soar
I left them all unaware that then
I echoed Mary's Amen.

War: 1944–45, Ireland

Tell the children, tell the children
Tell them that there isn't any bread
In the cupboard, or there won't be.
Tell them there's a war on
That Hitler started it all
And set them off with no shame at all.
Tell them that the queue is long
And people weary with no song.
Tell them that I'll write to De Valera
And ask him if he hasn't "era"
Loaf to spare now that he's in.
We voted for him. What a sin!
Tell them, tell them   the queue's moving
Up a little. Mind the shilling.

War: 1944–45, Ireland (Version 2)

Tell the children, tell the children

tell them that there isn't any bread

and there won't be, and I dread

to hear their cries. Say the wren

whose little stomach half a crumb would send

into fullness is cold like lead.

Yes he's dead, all dead, dead, dead

and he'll not scale the housetops again.

Tell them over   it's the war

Tell them, tell them   tell them   tell them

that it's bound to leave a scar.

Tell them they must learn to

empathize the victims, though it jar

and them to bitter memories condemn.

The Birthing

A void twixt me, creation intervenes
fair fields are full but barns are bare.
My hand is stayed. I know not where
to seek that I may find the poet's plough.
Perhaps a prayer will plead, give ointment to my pen
and shoot it at soul's bidding across the arid lines.
I should essay: "O thou Magnificatrix,
Divinest poet, from whose living pen
flowed full freely sad sweet song,
that of itself thee blesses, sans deeds,
magnify this lead. Ask Him for wine.
Do you well forth the water.
I'll be the stone."

Distractions

There are taverns on the road to the well,
sweet, seducing is to quaff of what they sell.
Minutes steal the rounds of hours
while the taverns wield their powers.
Bell calls halt before I sight the well.

Sweet Sixteen

He was tall, in kissing facile.
I was short, sixteen, unkissed.
He never guessed I'd be so agile.
He was tall, in kissing facile.
I said good-night, he answered nil
but spread his arm, then felt a fist.
He was tall, in kissing facile.
I was short, sixteen, unkissed.

Heart

What is this heart, this heart of mine?
Vineyard from whence comes the wine
that winds for me the wheel of life
in world where death of sin is life.

What is this heart, this heart of mine?
"Give-take-it-back-again" line, no spine.
See-saw swayed by every breath,
cringing, crying at a threat.

What is this heart, this heart of mine?
Chapelled casket, when the swine
are hunted home to howling hells
and sorrow salty subtlety knells.

Emily Dickinson

She closed the door and opened a drawer
then started to write in her virginal bower.
Emily Dickinson.
She wrote every day, never got any pay,
in her lace-curtained room with its disarray.
Emily Dickinson.
She penned pads to Higginson,
begged his views upon
Emily Dickinson.
She sidled away to a room of clay.
Left her disarray an eternal lay.
To Emily Dickinson.

Satan in Satin

Change an "a" in satan to an "i"
and you have satan in satin.
Now satan in satin combs the world
with a baton
and a line or two of Latin.
We see the satin, hear lofty Latin,
Sine (without) satan or the baton
but satan is subtle in satin.
He'll not give the satin and the Latin
Sine satan and the baton.

Christmas, 1956

Old wrinkled women wag
their nearly centuried heads
over Hungarian Headlines
and speak in wisdom-painted words:
"Don't know what the world is coming to."

The children, wide-eyed,
wondering, scarcely reasoning yet
halt suddenly wild capers
'round a Christmas tree to wisely say:
"We know What's coming to the world."

Thirty-One

There is nothing to show for the year
Save gray hairs spotting the near black
And the rolls of half-way flesh
At the mean, above, and below
True, there's the dress still on   still worn and worn
And within thoughts of piled-up years
With the same repetitions of sin on sin
Retreats, conversions and then the return
To begin again the old lie, relive the old show.

Oh God where is your Thunderbolt?

Odyssey '66: The Man I Killed[2]

"Fifth, thou shalt not kill"
"Just War; Self Defense; Execution of a Criminal."

Which was it? Denis Hurley says all three.[3]
But then it wasn't his bullet   no, mine.
After, I went back to see the marks:
Three there were, just under the crucifix too.
Strange. That it should be three and there.
But they were Hurley's bullets. Mine found
A softer rest. Right in the head. (I was
Always a good shot even at sixteen)
"Instantaneously." (like Kennedy in Dallas,
And me the Oswald) John Barry that said
Doc Reilly said it. He came after we walked
Away, just like that. Nobody stopped us.
Ye see, himself, the man I killed I mean,
Was R.I.C.[4] big brass   but no Kennedy he.
That was enough for them. I wonder how
His wife took it and is she still alive?
Now, stop man.

That was fifty years ago.
They're all dead now, 'cept me and Hurley.
Suppose he got me first. Poor Mary!
What would she have done.
No use thinking of that now.
She's gone too. Just war   ach,[5] it wasn't just
From the start. Eight hundred years' head start they

13

Had on us and all the time hell slaughter.
Just? No, not just! Unjust just and us the ones in hell.

But it's all over now   bar the six counties.
God help us, we'll never get them now.
Mick Kelly was right; we should never have given in.
I wonder if the bullet hurt   he dropped
Like a stone   a lump on the back of his head.
Oul' Breege Murphy that told me that:
Felt it, says she, layin' him out in the barracks,
No cleanin' up, says she, not like others
I've done. Clean shot.
Thou shalt not   just war   just.

II

He never knew who I was. If he did
That was the end of me. So it was self
 Defense too. Look how he finished Hegarty
And the Burkes and the others. No mercy.
And Hegarty's wife near her time too and
Him raisin' ten others. I remember
The mornin' we found him, the frost white on
His coat, and the hand stark and stiff still holdin'
The shovel. They said 'twas a job to put him
In the coffin. (They got one for him.)
We didn't wait to see. Himself (that was
Before I killed him) was out roamin' that
Mornin' with a hundred of them. That was
When they got the Burkes   Tom and Con and the
youngster.

A sore loss to the Unit that   shot
Down in the kitchen, the old mother there.
"All me boys," says she, and the tears wouldn't come.
The old man was white in the mornin' like
Snow at Christmas and never spoke after
to the day they closed the lid on him.
Then there was the burnin'; the old thatch went
Like smoke, even in the rain. They told me
All this after. We were out at Hegarty's.
No doubt he'd have got me then with the least
Suspicion. Aw but the pity that I got him
Before we started reprisals. That would
Have madded him. Two to one. A smart move that,
And we always did it, and later, three to one.
I can see him dancin' with rage at their
(Ours really, you know) genteel mansions puffin' up.
Self-defence it was and to be sure   Right
Through the head. A sharp sting, the surgeon told me,
And then my God! His God! The man I killed
Meetin' his God and mine. Goin' to Mass he was
(Not a Hamlet time) on the steps of the church
Under the crucifix and when I pulled the trigger
(Knowin' I was) I swear there was only
The three of us in it: God above, His
Blessed Mother and myself. And then there was
Him. The man I killed now, there lyin' waitin' not waitin.'
Then I said to the three of us, if it
Wasn't him, it was me, and we walked off.
Meetin' his God on the steps of the church
I left him, not me. Then I saw Hurley.
 "Good clean shot," says he, "and you got him,

A credit to the Column, they'll send it to HQ."[6]
Him on the steps meetin' his   "Thou shalt not…."
Stop it man! Self-defence it was, it was
Ó Anach Cuain[7] poor human condition *ag síleadh súl:*
hic sunt lacrymae rerum (in *Éirinn,* too, O Virgil)
The "still sad music" of self-defense,
Of Irish self-defense
"The unfettered control of Irish destinies"
Says I to Hurley and he nodded.

III

"Guilty m'Lord," says he when he opened his eyes
And he wasn't (the *Sassanach*)[8] in Ireland no more.
Criminal Execution of a, one R.I.C. officer, XX.
And I did it, a good clean shot,
No blood bedad, says Hurley
They said his wife never got over it. God help her,
Poor woman. I often wanted to go see her after.
Mary said it would ease my mind if I did.
Then when we had the money it was too late
And their children all gone to America.
I'll be soon seein' them now answerin' charges.
A good clean shot, no bloody blood says Hurley.
His scaffold the steps of the church where he
Went to Mass and the altar every Sunday.
He did. I saw him myself: the only time
We'll get him, and you and Hurley do it,
Says the OC[9] curtly. You be responsible: he's
Been warned he's goin' too far says he to me
Later   as we crouched   me and Hurley in the ditch

By the church waitin' in seven hours' dew, our feet
In the water I reviewed the review:
Curfew at seven, the children and old men
Behind locked doors with lists on the back;
"All males who appear in public with
Hands in their pockets will be shot at sight;"
And "because of attacks on the Crown Forces"
Field Marshall Lord XX, Lord Lieutenant of Ireland
Says "Martial Law": lettin' us die in our homes
No priest or doctor because "servants of the Crown"
Meet force (for a change) for force.
So himself   the man I killed   carries out Field
Marshall Lord X's, Lord Lieutenant of. . . .
(Ach no, my Lord   not Ireland now my Lord
Read the Proclamation, time for it now my Lord
"We declare the right of the people of
Ireland to the ownership of Ireland"
Read on, my Lord   and now my ex-Lord,
NO, we are not destructed yet; come to the names
Of the men that are dead now for proclaiming
Ireland Ireland's) orders to the yea yea yea
Of the Auxies[10] marchin' the streets at nine
And the rumble of lorries on the Dublin road
Of lorries and Tans   of lorries and Tans   and guns.
Execution of   orders   of criminals now
Remember my ex R.I.C. officer
The night old Pa Gilligan died. Young John
Went out after dark, a white flag high in
His hand, homemade with the brush and a towel,
In the light at the corner he fell
Blood-patchin' the poor hopeless symbol

Of peace for a shroud on the street, his father
Supine at home waitin' the priest. They left him
There till at dawn his mother found him
(All night they held her, wouldn't let her out)
And old Pa went without knowin'
Criminal it was   and you at the top. "Twas better I
Got you then   Execution of   an order
Of an R.I.C. officer,   of a criminal."

IV

"Guilty me Lord," I say, "but READ THIS FIRST."

Sonnet for Pearse: 1916–1966

No more 'tis to do for now 'tis done.

And God, of course, we'll win: unless the grain

Falling, die, itself   You said   remains alone.

Pearse here, my Lord! My death will not in vain

Have been? Lord, see! My army man-meal cut

Down, before its prime, with youthful zeal

Offering first fruits, whole burnt. Forever shut

To them now life where they set the seal

Of freedom. Well have they understood this

Your strangest of strange evangels: life in death.

You won't forget, my Lord, that other promise?

The hundredfold: to men who with "greater love" abet

Yet one more of your stern and strange commands:

Leave all   father, mother, brothers, sisters, lands.

Perspective: 1916–1966[11]

Rebellions are strange   and strange   not cheap.
I mean you know the one we had in Ireland
Just half a century ago.
All we wanted was to get what was ours:
Ireland for the Irish "from the sod to the sky."
Strange, how people you'd think knew better
Balk when it comes to some things.
There they were in Ypres
Fighting the Germans for Serbia
While at home in their own backyard
Another small nation (the "province" conscripted)
Not seeking justice from Nazis
Shouted wrong to the winds.

Odd it was to be sure. What can you say for them
But the old habit was hard to break
Though break it must. That was set down
When Pearse knelt long one night before he knew

And swore he'd die for Ireland:
One man enough, sang Mac Dara.

Yes, rebellions are strange and   oh dear!   dear.
Imagine the price of a capital in smoke.
"Nothing like it since Moscow," and Plunkett in the GPO
Beamed round at eyes tired wondering under raised brows
Not remembering Buonaparte.
Ach *delenda est Dublina*[12] now!
For slavery's worse than blood or flames
And revolution outruns reform long-promised
Lagging in the steps of fingers in pies more public.
So 179 buildings redden the sky Monday to Saturday
And her name becoming splendid among cities
A city, stopped   no bread or milk since Sunday
Revolves on relief slow.

There was death to pay too:
Men going home careless   no Rising at Fairyhouse
And women suffering in empty homes, careful
Closing windows waiting their men and boys
Meet the chance bullet all the same.
1,351 killed or severely wounded: *vide* statistics *á la*
Caulfield
To say nothing of casualties.
And after of course quick death for the wise
Fools who knew they were fools
Convinced that sacrifice is necessary, inevitable, useful
To right a wrong, make Gaels of West Britons
Even at cost (for one) of court-martial in bed

And, death's second aim, not fumbling now
Usurped (like rebellion home rule) its proto-claim.

Yes, someone seated blinded silent, paid:
Spoke loud with others when staccato, deafening,
For them penultimate   clicks
Fear-raising, were drowned by thundering echo:
"We hereby proclaim the Irish Republic
As a Sovereign Independent State."

Strange, too, I mean you know, it worked.

To Swift: Birthday Toast, 1967
(from "one quite indifferent in the cause.")

Now Jonathan, you won't believe it,
'Pon my word then do receive it
The proper word in proper place
I'm trying to set, in this mad race
To toast for you a proposal
Modest, you know, just like a pal.
And Jonathan, the task is hard
Since Muses now aren't mod   they're barr'd
And no one ever woos them to
Pour in the spirit   'cept it's dew
And mountain, too, tho' not Parnassus
Just think of that! By Jove! Good Gracious!

Here's to you, Dean, Doc, Gull and Drapier,
Our first Parnell   of Diamond rapier:
To Bickerstaffe, fine, mad astrologer
Who made poor Partridge look codologer;
To all you wrote for Whig or Tory
Redounding unto John Bull's glory,
To stop a war, renew religion
For which you never got a fig, Jon.
Now who but you could have a tub
Tell on a tale that raised hubbub
And caused all over such a clatter
It made Queen Anne say "What's the matter?"
Or what divine could e'er reflect
Upon a broomstick with effect
So true, so holy, so   elect!
Then there was of course your Stella
To whom the journal went to tell a
Tale of dreary London daily
What you did, do, sad, mad, gaily.
And as for her you named Vanessa,
Well, all we'll say is, "May God rest 'a."
No point asking any questions
Too many ready with suggestions
To fill lacunae on your two suns.
Yes, here's to you, Doctor, noble Dean
Who could at will upset a Queen
Or tell a tale of such adventure
That children gape while adults censure.
I wonder what your thoughts are now
On Yahoos and their kind below
As like good Troilus you look down

Laughing, no doubt, while wise men frown.
And where's your *saeva indignatio*[13]
'Gainst men capable of *ratio*?
Love him by divine *ukase*[14]?
Not just Peter, John and Thomas?
Too, what about your politicians?
Whig or Tory? Or is there fissions?
Does one merely cross the floor
To find they're mix'd not two no more?

Now Dean, forgive my list of queries;
They're just rhetoric   nothing serious.
And if there's an'thing here objectionable

It's that I'm like your own dear Lemuel.
Once more again here's to you, Dean
Three hundred years   your name still green!

Conservative

He walked with measured pace
And when he talked
His Mona Lisa smile
Switched on between the paragraphs pared
With voice monot'oned.

I wondered was he ever
Fully stretched
Would he let them at him (self)
As he walks on Corridors of Power
Does he doodle at meetings?
Has he ever
Looked at Sandy Shaw[15]
Heard "Puppet"
And does he think on minis—
That they're here.
IS he ever?
Or has he lived in twilight zones
Refusing *nuestro mundo*[16] *stimulessence*
Has he never
Sturmed und Dranged[17]
Through years of bulging body
And/or gawking adolescence
Or was the Mona Lisa always there
Feline, waiting to slick on/off
At corners and at paragraphs and sentences?

Morning Train Journey

They always sit
With their stale faces
And closed eyes

The morning after
And (now) it's high knees and red shoes
With leather coats and the fur and the boots.

Some read the papers
Yawning.
Gootcha choo
Gootcha choo
Goo-choo
Goo-choo
Goo-choo

And the dame with the Eastern eyes
Unfriendly
Closes them again
To the goo-choo, goo-choo
Lilt of the puff-puff.

Two men with scarves talking
Putting down newspapers
After the sports page   Quiet.
And the girl with the red check cape
Not coat (it's tight at the hips)
And too big legs
Eats a square of Cadbury's
From a bulging bag in black leather
With a comb at the top.

And I wonder if
With the *flúirseach* flow of the *LSD*[18]

And the boots and the fur
And the Cadbury's
If (I say if) we the stale faces
Are satisfied.

Vocation

"By the rood!" they said NO:
"Let him stay now;
Long enough gone from us,
And besides   They're all pagans beyond
Like to kill him this time (for escaping)."
Relations and friends of *Calphurnius*[19]
At *Bonaven Taberniae*[20] long ago,
Advising.

"Tempting fate."
"Stay at home."
"Your father is old and Conchessa is ready to go."
But "by the rood,"
Maun[21] is not Maun now but Patrick
Anointed
Called to change, as saints must, human life.

So he went, alien
He, leavening, transforming, self-spending, kindling

Cunning of Druids
To strike Tara's[22] fires not for Baal now but Christ
Flame eternal at home
And beacon the way to the now of alien shores.

Chairwoman

De gustibus non est disputandum[23]
And all that
And me, I can stand em
A lot less garrulous

I'd want her to catch her breath
And rest and listen and wait
To engage brain more
Before operating tongue

We don't expect her infallible tongue
To be infallible
But she plays God   like
(Though I must say from what I've noticed
He elects more often than not
The delicate divinity
Of silent infallibility)
And goes on and on and on
Forever   with no   Amen

As I said above, *De gustibus* etc.

But again, to recap
Give me a chair
Who can listen to the meeting
And with ear in silence
Tuned   use the brains
Engaged, linked and operating
Towards production

Hound

Why are You always asking
                God
That other thing
Just when I've after given You
That other thing
Must You always be asking
              God
One more
Can't You stop when You've hunted me
And let me pant
For just a bit
Knowing that
That panting is just a prelude
And that there'll be more panting
(And puffing too)
Before long

Don't You remember that last time
When I said NO
And You hunted me
And wouldn't let me go

And after the yes
There was more

And now it's this that and that
Other (thing) again
And You're catching up
And I know I'll be caught
For at my back I always hear
Not time's winged chariot but

YOU

You Hound

II

Stop it for God's sake God
And let my world go round
And round
The mulberry bush maybe
But let it go

And let me be

ME!

Dying

I've thought about dying, living,
And wondered how it'd come
"Stalking in chambers" to find me
Walking in halls
Sleeping gone to bed at ten
Not waking
In creeping cancer days
Tired of pain and hemlock
And wishing
Or on the road jolted looking at clouds moving
From life to life not breathmeal
But breathing the last breath into other life sudden
What last face will bright the dark under lids sealed
What sound last heard will echo in chambers tuning in to
ever
What me stopped in second parturition
Will meet the mystery
And after dark be dazzled into now?

Yes, I've thought about dying, living,
With all these thoughts
And somebody calling death leveler
And Hamlet saying *the readiness is all*

And as I wondered, wandered

And now I have to go and eat my supper.

GRINGA TO GRINGOS: Up to San Luis Potosí (Mexico)

We stopped at Querétaro
Más o menos
(More *más*, than *menos*)
A half-hour for lunch.
Muy caliente
Los maseros rushing
Blind to waving hands
And eyes seeking and watching
El chofer y la sobrecargo swallowing.

Waiting, remembering
The just-now *sanitario* full
And smelling not like *los cerros*
Y el camión Tres Estrellas de Oro
With air-conditioning on
And after, looking.
Re-tasting too-hot-for-tourists
Enchiladas, rinsed cold with *una coca*.
Walking the *más-o-menos-más*
Hot half-hour on concrete.
¡Mira! ¡De colores!
Past the orange-clad *hombre*
Sweeping tourist (*y otro*) trash.

I spilt *nieve* (*choc-o-la-te*)
On my dress, gray.
(Double-knit it'll wash out when I get back.)
Looking. *Estanquillos* with
Cajetas, ponchos, and *Valsequillo* onyx

Muy caro, amigo
Wait till Puebla and Santa Ana.

II

Boarding again to the strains of
"El Barquito" y "el anuncio de coca cola."

Remembering and seeing more
Women at streams, rubbing on rocks
Their rainbow wash.
And once   *¡Qué linda!   una muchacha* shampooing
(*Otomies* maybe, of the valley of the Mezquital,
"Adapting to their harsh environment.")

Men behind oxen yoked in pairs
Or ones when burros or vacas foraged

Among *rocas, grandes y muchas.*
Later when valleys were green
Los hombres following *caballos*
Blue and orange sometimes on the horizon
With *las mujeres* behind scattering.
Or *todo el mundo* sitting.

(Here, I mused, *al fresco,*
Todos los días)
"The pause that refreshes"—cokeless!
And no *siesta* supine
Like *Querétaro* road-menders.

III

Y en qualquier lugar las magueyes
"Exhaustively exploited"
Profuse in "soil of pronounced aridity":
Aguamiel: ¡olé! Tequila tourist
Pulque: to drink, *a la casa*
Ixtle: metamorphosed to bags
That tote your *curios*
Y cositas.

And everywhere, horizoning
Los cerros
Majestic, pristine
Untouched save where
Echevarría   Arriba!
Sent satellites high to paint him
White and monstrous
On screens the gringos missed
Proclaiming Pepsi
"Todo es más sabroso. . . ."
 Y coca
"El chispa de la vida"
Disfrute, amigo!

I remember now *la mezquite*
Taller than Texan
The yucca strong and alone
And cactus, piped and organed   adapting
Fenced round *las chozas*
De los campesinos, sombreroed.
And on *nuestro Tres Estrellas*

Shy, soft-voiced, not intruding
"¿Gusta café o refresco?"
Y escrito en blanco
"Cierre bien la puerta—gracias"
Y "No suba Ud. Los pies, aquí"
¡Por favorcito!

Pero siempre
I remember
Los cerros y los cerritos
Brown and dry and hard and high
Among *curvas, peligrosas y muchas*
Horizoning a dynasty
Back there up to San Luis Potosí.

STASIS

She died today at five
She stopped, ceased, no IS, no more
The sun not seen
Not light nor you, nor me
But dark or void or nothing?

(What IS that nothing?)
The tick-tock dial told me tomorrow you
But she (an IT now?)
Nor hears its constancy
Nor sees a morrow in her now.

The wind blows trees as yesterday
While she numbs through our time oblivious
Nor feels its harsh unkindest cut.
What un-nature, unearth now draws or repels
And what of mind and wareness
Knowing the knowledge she knew
Does she know now she knows or knows not?
Where is that un-beinged being
By hand or eye or ear unreachable
What does it know
What hasn't it come to know?
She died today at five
ALL that's body, mind
The things we know
Or think we know.

The rest is God.

INVITATION, 1972

What are you doing up there Mary
And the world the way it is
Why doesn't the God your Son
Incarnate you for a while
And give us a Second Coming
A Parousia to rouse

Up Pilates to kill him again in you
And save this new roaming world
Of pills and atoms and pushbutton earthquakes
And just plain old institutions
That crush the soul of mod
Lepers and blind beggars
That cry and can't see trees as men.
We need recharging
To hear again from God
That it's He that
Stops the copters falling
Makes grass grow (green)
And decks communes with hippies
Love if not lily lorn.
Put on your *Fiat*
And let it be
And hurry
For we've ways
To make more lepers and blind beggars
With lunar speed
And when you come
You'll have to come to Bethlehem
By Astrojet
And don't forget
To find a runway
Where we won't dispose of you (*quietly*)
Before you touchdown.

FRIEND

We you and We
Me to You and You to me
 In joy and tears
We laugh   We
Because
(Y)our problem's gone
That job is done
And so we're glad We
We laugh and then We
And then We cry We
My God! I can't go on
This is the straw
Too much
Not God can ask me this
And listening You absorb my tensions
And soon our sorrow metamorphoses
And there is joy in tears
Being there One
And then We carnival
Nor joy nor tears but We
In song balloon and dance
And rollercoaster careening
Living high pitch We
Carnivaling We
Nor You nor I but We
Nor I nor You but We
And then We silent We
Listening

Knowing We're there
When nor You nor I perhaps not knows
Listening
When not to say
Is shouting
We listening We
Knowing

There
We there We
We
In laughter tears and carnival
We
In silence

We

You We I We

Here

RUDE

I met a rude man this morning
Ugh! *malvado*!
You . . . "put me in my place"
And forever etched for me
What NOT a gentleman is.

Where eons tick as yesterdays
And I AM
(Y tú tambien—que lástima—y tú!)[24]
I'll meet you
Across myriads of minds
And remember you incarnate
BOOR
Your studied casual cutting eyes and tongue
And shout then as now
"This merits but oblivion"
And wish I were
Less like an elephant and a Christian
To forget and not pity

black friday: the SUPREME decision January 1973

had 1873 god-like
decided the question
as 1973
you'n me might not even
have reached the trash can
for how could they've got
moms 'n dadsjustlikethat
they not having reached the trash can either

nature *envoi* to abortee:
monstrosity man-ated
where west and east are one
in limboed light life-less
eclipse is for after
when having risen and risen
the horizon is westward
not east nor west for you
you two-backed monster
death-in-life
to   with you.

Birthdays

They are yesterdays

And we look to the next

For between there is only

the now

On the birthday there's

The last and the next

The link with before the first

The promise of after the last

when now is

With nor first nor last nor next

and being is birthday

In the Traffic on Fredericksburg Road

In the mirror the faces behind
Beard and eyes restless
After the green light honking
Another: hippie-like
Thinking into the windshield
I start as my wheels
Joggle over the yellow catseyes
And then it's a tired blond
Staring
At the light caressing sprayed hair
Pursing lips
To massage the lipstick line
Straight
For a rendezvous (I think)
With a someone
A husband or herself
I hear horns as her mirror's face honks
And his and his
Next a head hairless
Easter egg with a face
Old
I wonder about
Standards and the Department of Public Safety
Then my Texaco comes

And I swing left
Get a "fill'er up with regular"
And ease out into
The again
Mirror faces

Commitments

Our commitments make us
Not make other commitments
It's because (it's to you) I promised
And said yes
That I'll stay
And won't walk out
When there's an option of othering
At horizons beyond the here

The first commitment narrowed options
Not being then
Or being, not presented
And now (that) they're here
And I'm committed
What's to do but pass
Or let pass to where choices can be

For what have we more with each other
Than our word

POWS

Pouring back from alien lands
Into us
Is it alien to alien
I ask myself

Can they ever come back
How do you pick up the threads left hanging
In the middle of a summer afternoon
As if there were no years between
With all man life
And foreign eyes
And blood and maryjane
And limbs less 1 or 2
Trunks transported
And time clocked by dull thuds and sirens
Punctuating advances retreats
And my-lai's world-viewed
And in compounds herded
Where hours are years (now)
And years are days (after)
Now they're back after Paris
With papers plans and puttering
To TV receptions where the whole world can see
THEY'RE BACK

Intuition

in the end I said
I'm right!
shouting it in me
after the two psychologists
gave all the reasons
1-2-3-4 etcetera
(an' i agreed)
why the whole structure was in-, de-, un-, not human

(in the real sense of the word)
and I remembered all the times
in me I fought me
me welling up in me rebelling
against the 1-2-3-4's etc. around me
me not finding 1-2-3-4 etc. answers
but knowing like I always do

there was something phoney about their 1-2-3-4's etc.
and because I wasn't a psychologist
or on the way
(Ph.D. candidate) maybe
nobody was interested in listening to my rebellion
but it didn't matter
and it doesn't now
and I won't even say it

except to myself
for I'll know when it happens again
(and it will)
and it is
that   I'm   still   right

Fragment at Morning

I always wanted to write
A poem
About the way things go
Through my mind
Wondering when I wake up enough
To try to remember
If I dreamed
About me with a horse's head
And you a lion poised
Ready
Or sensing a nightmare
From the taste in my mouth
Brushing remembrance into my teeth
Living again the epilepsies
Of a something aborning
In sealed walls with no light
Except the fear searchlighting
My eyes into shock
Coming back to

"The sound of beautiful music"
And "the KQXT time is 6:29"
And here is a brief summary of
You'd better hurryup or you'll be late again
At Mass undulating
To the once upon a time *kyrie eleison*

From the now lord have mercy struggling at the throat

After a dry monstrance
Eating the Body of Christ Amen
My God I believe
Help Thou my unbelief
And *ite missa est*
And go down moses
Down *deogratias* for the coffee
Remembering the gospelizing
Neighbor who got up
In the night to loan a loaf
Good Samaritan
And hop back again
Are they protestants or catholics
Samaritans
"Proddie proddie on the wall
Ate a loaf and then they fall
When the devil rings the bell
All the proddies go to . . . "
And the catholics come tumbling after

Bell   hell   well   well
Time   time   time   for my books
These are my books   these are my books

I never travel without my books
We'll start with metaphors this morning class
Or wouldn't meteors be even better
With the little prince
Better resume that later
And now to   bed
Metaphors I mean
Metaphysics   metanoia   metamorphose   meta me
An example
O yes
My head is split   ing

Of Course I Think

About the meaning of me

First: there's the me
              I easily see
              in the mirror
              or in parts
              and in part
              looking down

Second: there's the me
              that seems to converge
              in my head
              to direct operations
              right over the eyebrows

and in a little

Third: there's the me
that reaches back to origins
and out to beyonds
where this me
and originator are one
in some non-time non-world
but definitely not non-me
and excuse me but
somehow
in fact by now
this me
is all three
in a way I can't explain
though the books call my whole me
spirit mind and body
I get quite confused
with their footnotes and crossreferences
about how the three me's
make me act like I do
and it's always simpler
for me (the middle me)
to return
to my own explanations
and not get too curious
as they would have me
about which me
makes me do what

Present Shock: Autobiography (or Living: Autobiography)

home is a place to leave   I think
but my grandmother says to love
some things used to stay the same like mothers and
sometimes fathers
I only remember my first mother and father
in love back in Cleveland Ohio
before mother and me moved to Texas with a new father and
other kids
and after we moved again   mother and me   to Oklahoma
with only a father (and no kids)   who mother said   loved
me very much
until the day my first father came and took me with him
to another mother a real one he said (and more kids)
and I stayed there till my grandmother my first one I mean
came with her new husband in a cadillac
and took me   where she said   I'd really see what love is

and that's where I am now
thinking
about home being a place to love and some things staying
the same
like my grandmother says

wondering

if I should go back to college after christmas and get culture
not semester hours like the others
like she says
or just hang around airports

Future Shock

Nothing is   only change   anymore permanent
computers combining comfortable
knowledge into nuances
never known   nerve-knocking
eachday relationships
more temporary tenuous each day
the man in 48 gone to Alaska
not expecting ever to return
except maybe to pop in next year on a charter
home is a place to leave
just like that
the bank a remnant of permanence
at the corner demolished
and in a week
an instant
pre-fabbed
plugged-in
clipped-on
Modulared
for you anachronism
round-the-clock permanent staffs

rewriting telephone directories

permanents computerizing impermanents

permanence is dead

no one expects longterm anything

stays   encounters   commitments

all temporary tendril-ly tenuous

we're future shocked

in too much change

in too little time

we patent production of plastic people

with bodies disposable

hearts transplantable

kidneys willed

noses nuanced to a neatness not noticed

skins tinted to taste

each dawn success percentages rising

with now the ultimate:

tinkering with intellect in test tubes

to say nothing of DNA molecules

and then

who'll decide who'll be Xeroxed

the Einsteins

us   the plebians   us

a couple of each

why not? a "proper" à-la-who? proportion

who'll decide who'll be ripvanwinkled

at freezing point

to 2070, 80 or 90?

from the choices we choose a tomorrow world

carbonned

computerized
controlled
disposable
plasticized
replaceable
trade-in
in a word instant
but already, and *hic sunt lacrymae rerum*[25]
can't you hear the whispering responses
humanity in still sad music *ag síleadh súl*[26]
looking in loneliness
in commune couplings looking
in plasticized loneliness
exhausted looking
looking returning to yesterday
returning to yesterday looking
for LIFE looking
for LOVE looking
looking

College English: The First Year, 1973

sometimes i wonder
if i just shouldn't
give up with a whimper

and let the buttons take over
it's still a thinking operation

to write a paragraph or two
it won't happen when you switch to on
or up the volume
you see in sentences you need
(generally that is)
a subject and a verb
with an object or two occasionally

(and then there's a way or two of swapping them to get

variety)

it's as difficult as that
and then of course there's the WHAT
problem after you know the HOW
or while you're knowing it even
that *nemo dat quod non habet*[27] bit
and when you just can't sit with a book
or you haven't gone beyond the tube
or your in-general surroundings
for matter
and your own internal revenue is pretty low
or exhausted
or out of order
through neglect
or non or mal use or whatnot
then of course you can't can you

it's a problem
perhaps we don't need to produce any more
writers of sentences or paragraphs
and perhaps on today's scene
the essay

that antipode of instantomatic culture
is altogether for the birds
aristophanic or other
in The Age of Transition:
From Writing to Non-writing:
1946-1996
as the aural-oral historians
will be taping in 2073
and writing will be
caviar to the general

who knows
but *noblesse oblige* or it used to
an pore lil ole english teacher that i am
i can't help wishing
that somehow somewhere someone
would find a compromise
in hiatus 73
between the medieval essay-ism
of the forties and after
and   the i don't know what of
the i don't know when
but now birthing tomorrow

Morning in Ireland

I wonder what the two black crows
        are saying up there
        in the tall tree
        just inside the gate

the others are consistently chorusing
        cawcawing
from tree to tree
but the pair, philosophic
        are deep in dialogue
        importuning
maybe it's freedom and responsibility
self-image   future shock   and current crises
they're about
but if you ask me
(*not mindin' me own bizness*)
I'd say they're just taking a lookdown
at the town
from their *comme-il-faut* for crows[28]
conspectus
and wondering if that young scamp
with the peaked cap
and the catapult
before he leaves them alone
is going to take a cockshot or two
up at them
in a few minutes

"Not a Sparrow…." (*Matthew 10:29-31*)

the storm blew the old tree down last night

some of us heard a thud around four

and turned over and snuggled down under

      in the morning we looked

still gaunt it was

broken   beside its gaping entrails

lying now   low   bereft of power

gently having bowed down and out

inching past classrooms 5A and B

to fall innocuous and clean

on this side of the electric wires

      with uncertain leverage

swaying

it might have died here on us

or on "the link"

or on St. Anthony's

or on Paddy's place

or any other arc of that 360°

Encounter

suddenly it was spring and you

and when we talked

the words were props

on which to lean   not dwell

the ones not said

more palpate   unincarnate

like spirit things

felt   not thinged

(and like Keats' unheard melodies, sweeter)

and when you went

on   to talk   to do   to things

I wanted to have gone with you

not there

but driven to the edge of the world

forever

Train Trip, Ltd.

If you go from Dublin west to Ballyhaunis of a spring morning you are likely
to come across surprises all with limited perspective that make you wonder
what the whole picture is from a plane maybe or living close up.

I saw   a path between daffodils cornering round a house
                  whose face I'll have to conjure up
                  a longbilled bird rising out of the bog

                  frighted by noise flying nowhere and back

I never saw   the heads of the field of mottled calves
                  fralloping through the hedge disturbed at morning
                  mooning

I watched   and over the Shannon
                  more and more stone walls parallel   square
                  rectangle   up
                  green brown and purple patches
                  big little and inbetween

                  stretching out up into sky

I wondered   where the young traveling pair were going in
                  Castlerea
                  with their yellowred cart with flowers on the side
                  he holding the horse at the railway crossing
                  and she tidying up cans looking in at us smiling

                  what would win at Naas on Saturday
                  "7 to 4 on" or "the outsider 8 to 1" that the two
                  uniformed station men dialogued engrossed on
                  the train heaved out and I'll never know now

if he "made it to *Fairyhouse*[29] Easter Monday"

I waved   at hills and tree groves
some spot among which   seated   walking   talking
thinking   silent
is a friend I want to stop off and see

and now it's Ballyhaunis and off:
"Take it easy"
"That step is high"
"Watch it now"
"That's right"
"There we are"

Home: three dimensional   perspective unlimited
no surprises close up

Peace

UNLESS I'm still within
happy to be: thus and there and here
it isn't mine   evading me
aching after other   time place person
sitting on edge   for whatever cause
not fully living the now
nor patiently pursuing patterns
inevitable here

how can I then   not full
share with you   him   her
to give and live
the second command
and prove I know the first?

unchecked within
the ache absorbing

wears   tears   sears
the source
consuming energy I should conserve
conducting Christ in me
of peace the prince
to you   and them

but after dissension
when unresenting
reborn once more and cleansed
when all desire is nil
with nor pursuit nor pursuer
when I am full
brimming over, pouring out gifts in me
bringing you stasis
then we both have peace

Anne Marie

she asked me to write a poem about her for school
but how can you write a poem on a 15-year-old
whom you see every 2, 3 or 5 years passing thru' Colonia,
New Jersey
from Ireland to Texas
on a long or short weekend
seeing the colt grow   longhaired   shining
(getting up early to have it washed for leaving)
suddenly appearing, smiling alive
disappearing
introducing her friends   shy
(she's a nun   she's in my room)

and calling Mom too late at night
to ask if she can stay over with Cathy or Stacey or whomever
and getting bawled out for it?
And hearing from Dad that she got caught smoking
in school corridors   a problem
Yes   how can you write a poem about one you don't know
save in glimpses more or less triennial   growing
remembering her the time before that last
in big white monstrous plaster casts hipbound
arrested on bed or floor or couch till awkward
someone responding, strong came, stooped to lift her up and
vary the perspective?
You can't you know, write a poem about her
you could guess or imagine or make up   just plain make up
but I think if you just-remember glimpses
and periscope them all together like this
and say this is it Anne Marie   this is it!
"it's more the thing that is."

Amiddening[30]

We were all there amiddening   all 52+ or -
Breathing for 2 weeks out
Germs that would forever never leave
The composition of 251 BEB the same
Resource for hunters 2076 maybe
Or can they (will they then if they can't now)
Midden out the CO_2
Sighed out in waves multiplied

By 52 more or less each day
With eachday variants of 2-3
At 7½-8 hour periods
Punctuated by breaks
Lunch, water and rest?

This poem could then be a finding aid:
Direction to middens
Atmospheric: concentrate on 251 BEB
With related areas   corridor   restrooms
Adjacent   and of course
Jester

Look for: coke-coffee-pepsi (diet!) clues
(Cross reference to sociologists: What do
Diet can middens tell about
'76 A.D. Texas High School
History et al. teachers' concern
For calorie intake?)

Then there were
The water drinkers
Bending over, filling up
Styrofoam etc. cups
For consumption inside

And after, latent doodlers
During sitaholic sessions
Sponging in
Expert concentrate Ph.D. knowledge
Poured out in over down around beside
Potpourri 12 nearly   days   in a row

I'll bypass the gum
Cigarette 'n' noise middens
But I can't end this without
A *hic jacet*[31] reference
To the tamale-beer-in-charade-Buda possibilities
A whole new vista
And the Barbeque Bones hickoried
In Coupland Inn

(For how would y'all   in   2076
ever know we even went amiddening
TEI borne thataway?)

To say nothing of the trip South chartered
Via Fredericksburg *fachwerk* with much *à pied*
To change forever there midden contours
And at Spanish missions
Renowned in San Antone

My last word
Honest!
Will be towards notebooks
Chuckfulled with   in Texas
Geography   geology   indians   botany

Archeology   spaniards   imperialism
Mexico   revolution   republic
State   antebellum conditions
Architecture   art   material
Slavery
And whatdeyaknow
Civil war!

Indiscriminate   beautiful   flowing over   exciting
Institute in
Good hunting   middenologist!
Texas Culture

Thanksgiving in Advent *(Jeremiah: 9, 10)*

Most vulnerable here   I lie

Supine I Lord

And tho I lie   have lied   Lord to me

You and I Lord both know
I have broken covenants
That had you framed me
Before your own enfleshment
Cursed would I be indeed
With men of Judah
Not hearing Jeremiah (angry for you)
Or having heard   unheeding
Pursuing the to be of
  wisemen glorying in wisdom
  strongmen in strength
  richmen in riches
Forgetting
You bringing and to bring to earth
     kindness
     justice
     uprightness
Most grateful now here bend I Lord
Still supine   vulnerable still

Waiting
Knowing alone   I still lie and not know
    that I'm not master
    nor can choose my course
    nor direct my step

For P.M.M. (at Christmas)

I love you

For only understanding the way I am

To just want to stand close

And let my one primeval roar

To ease Vesuvius in me towering

The ferment reflecting vistas

That encircle and surround

To suffocate to outpouring

Weaving avenues to rest

In your God and listening heart

Let Me Not Die

Let me not die till i have lived   God
what is to live
to live and love are one
to live's the same as
equal to   to love
to love other   like I love me
like I want for me
full   flowing   brimming   down to
to be   for other
encompassing
cushioning

not seeing   and seeing all
delighting in
waiting   seeking
to live is
all the while being not for me
    tip-toed
    poised
    to give

first   laying   down   life   piecemeal
till when
to live is
to love to fullness
and stop
and BE

If I Were God

if i were God
i'd brush everything under the carpet
looking down
demented nearly
at the mess we make
picayunish   poring
cutting up each other

in church

declaring we keep the first: "I believe in God"
outside
not even seeing the second: who IS my neighbor

yes i think that's what i'd do God
if i were you
tho' you could now point out to me
a thing or two i'd say
if you started

nevertheless   in my God moments
"made in your image"   i am

      i'd sweep it all away
and since you're God always
always to be depended on
now i say
i count on you doing the same

the way i am (free will)

thank you for taking me the way i am Lord
(not that i know how that is   always)
but i know you do
and who cares after that
i wonder though
do you even sometimes seeing my all

believe you made me yourself

come to think of it
if i made a robot
i'd understand it better than it
and stop all its nonsense when the crunch came
and save it
i'd have one over on you   wouldn't i
for it couldn't not do what i built in

i wish it were that way with me'n'you
so you'd be in control
or would it then not be me   "made in your image"
and i wanting the me you made me
and wanting you also to renege, unmake me, save me

eureka! that's it
like i told you
it's the way i am
and what are we gonna do

"Hic sunt lacrymae rerum" [32]

Sometimes I want to curl up
into a ball
scrunch up my heart to nothing

to not feel the pain
in my cocoon   hibernating forever

and then again
I want to stand astride
the four angels on the tower trumpeting
and roar my protest
at myself and you
and all the chalices
we lightly thrust at each other politely
fiercely   tersely   daily
with smile or shrug or eye or tongue
passing indifferently
to address our God

Facts

I don't know you God
or else
drawn into the current of your beatitudes
i'd float abandoned
to the breadth and depth and height
of your munificence
lightly burdened with the daily yoke and sweet

I don't love you God
or else
i'd stop the shilly-shallying
and in one big act of contemplation
live the love you launched

at Bethlehem or Calvary
and race my resurrection days
to where nor eye nor ear
can see or taste the what
you have for me

Prayer Now and in *Exodus: 17*

What were you doing   Moses
sitting on the rock
with your arms upraised
and Aaron and Hur holding them
when you got tired

What were you doing inside you   I mean
where you are all you   all together
that's what I want to know
while Israel fought Amalek till sunset
and you got tired standing cruciform
till upheld
Joshua mowed down Amalek
and his people at Rephidum
with the sword   two-edged
only one striking out from Joshua's strength

What were you doing   answer me
when you couldn't stand up

upraise your arms on your own

I think you could only dispose yourself
get ready
be   for God
to let Him *fiat* his act through you
gifting you
to double the edge on Joshua's needed blade

Prophet (After *Jeremiah*)

Why must I howl my days and years
To ear unheeding
Ministering   doom and gloom
In song of love
To desert airs
Now monstrous grown
With your ires divine
And promises   waiting
While blithely by
To festivals of new and gold calves
And foreign gods and women, wine and song
Your people orgy
The covenant   forgotten carefully
Until you weary
Urge Nebukkadnezzar on
Unrelenting
To make his *veni, vidi, vici* song
And bring them howling now
To knees and tears and years
In alien lands
Where Israel is scattered
And Judah but a memory

Of light and hope to purge desire alive
And make them cry
Yahweh, Yahweh,   Yahweh?

Yahweh's Song

Woe is me that I am God, not man
For you, Israel, my son, faithless
Chosen first and promised
In covenant with Abraham
I cannot now devour with sword or flame or lion's roar
Though you have raped me more than once
Stumbling in your sin:
In false heart
Bending low at Gilgal;
Espousing foreign lovers
From everywhere and nowhere
Bearing their harlot children;
And greedy you have ground my people down
To nakedness in hunger, cold and homeless;
My poor oppressed, you prosperous

Built barns to store the wine and oil
The grain, silver and gold
Gift and fruit of my bounty.

Yet woe is me, for I am Yahweh
I will save you
And bring you to straight paths
Where you will walk before me just
And be what you are: my people

For January 19, 1977

"It's the time you spend
with your rose that matters"
and I think that's why
I want to say I love you again
for being there with
outside of time
your presence gifting your present
like the sound of the sea
at the edge of the world
looking not surprised at me unclosing
as if you knew everything always
or yesterday or milenniums before we met
like God somehow
understanding what I don't myself
distanced   outside of   looking objectively
but from a universe of empathy and sympathy
that makes us one
showing me you

and when again again   and again
you spend time
it will be new and more
yet still the same
for we will have grown from each again
pregnant to birthing the rising vortex
widening towards new tomorrows
to a now of rest
knowing as we are known

Thinking

I don't know how I can put up with me Lord
If I didn't know you knew everything always
I'd be ashamed of me daily
What I keep reminding myself   I must
Is that You made me
You're to blame in a way for everything
I can't help me   sometimes
And sometimes I don't want to
It's just   too   much
That's where you come in
Take over   that's an order
Nor in order I admit
But what am I to do
I just can't help it
I'm only me
The me you made
I could go one way or another I know
If it's another   that's me too
    the truth
I wish I could be like all the saints
They just sound so good
Imagine that lil ole flower
Just always able to give up for you
If that's what you want, Lord, that's it
You've had it   *No puedo cierto*[33]
So just start all over with me
And lay out some other musts
Take Augustine
I haven't been through all he has
But I'd like to
Impossible I know   I'm just a woman
I am a woman
A woman I know
Is more than a man
Like your mother was more than you

Is that heresy
It's the truth and you are the truth
And I am made in your image and likeness
So I am truth
Sorry
I love you
Me
Amen.

Sounds

The last thing I heard in the series
Was me breathing
After the inevitable clock recurring
And the Broadway traffic
Undulating into
The twitter of three birds
Harmony-ing always background music
(distractions flowing in   Peter I love you
you too God   sorry for the sequence)
My trying ear interrupted too
With doors opened clicking closed
And somebody upstairs dropping a something
Heavy   moving
Sometimes like a stallion in spring
And a single voice soliloquying somewhere
Confidential
Was that a man raping
Our sacred Saturday convent morning
Slamming doors and his deep voice
Or a strange nun voice visiting
Altoing chit-chat loud in halls
Uncareful of silence and time
Pipes channeling rushed water
Obscurely in walls carrying surely
Morning's germs smoothly

Staccato intermittent intrusions
From I can't tell where   what   why   or   who
And me breathing quietly always at end
I listen for the sound of my blood coursing
That won't be heard
I listen for all my body working noiseless
But always it's the breathing
And my ear beginning all over again

passion sunday

to tell you how i felt
when you said
no I have no time (for you)
might take eternity
even if I could
or knew I wanted to

        you closed me surer
than fingers after heart
stopped dead in *rigor mortis*
and life has ebbed casual-like
leaving dead tissue

        and when now remembering
i imagine
how we might meet again
if sudden chance
diagonaled our parallels
i see me   iced   stopped dead
lips set   head caught erect
eyes staring   and not looking
unsure of wanting   willing
not able   absolutioning
to thaw towards you
and how we were

and
passing on to where i am

Archiving: monolog on me

i'm an ár-kə-vist
yes! ár-kə-vist
A-R-C-H-I-V-I-S-T
"Caviar to the general"
as witness overheard chit-chat
over fences friendly
"yes, we're having archivists for dinner tonight, thirteen"
"oh   and how do you fix 'em?"

(on parchment, i mused   looking on   listening in
acid free, water resistant, foil lining
and maybe marinated in spiders' webs in the dark
musty below basement level
with a sprinkle of dust
at sixty-eight or seventy degrees)

a what?
Yes an ár-kə-vist am i   am i
sprouted into archivism after umpteen years
of college english   high school principaling   and
french
and   what not

what's that?
an archivist is an archivist is an
official keeper of documents,   of records public and
unpublic

(chez nous)   calligraphing early Texas days of us
on horse and buggy
three black 'n' white French soeurs
sixty-niners stage-ing across prairies
from the "island city" emerging
to San Antonio aborning "city of the sun"
to start hospital operations
and the file of letters
that "rooted" my job.

Distractions at Oblate[34]

I
OMI Grotto, June 1, 1977
Contemplation on a Sparrow

The sparrow is a cheeky runt
Intruding bold on conversation
Building on a private lot
All set aside for contemplation

Of inhibitions he has none
His private life with animation
In *joie de vivre* he parades
Hopping in profound elation

I'm wondering if I'm very narrow
Watching a such exhibition
For wishing   once   to be a sparrow

II
At the Figtree at 42, OMI, June 2-3, 1977
The Bizzy Lizzard

The lizard long stands in a stance
His head caught in a looking dance
His tail goes back beyond his vision
And looking still, he sits back   wishin'?
Then suddenly he looks at me
(I wonder does he really see?)
And spreads along from snout to tail
And licks a stone and darts again
What is that motion up and down
He seems to make from chest to crown
Like pushups in a tough workout

(Except it doesn't wear him out)
Look there, he's pushing up again
Gyrating now in his head dance
He's circled round that figtree leaf

Darting towards his next dance stance
Strikes me the lizzard's a bit a wizard.

ROOTS: INCARNATING THE WORD IN TEXAS, 1869

In the beginning
Was the fever
Yellow   yellow   yellow
And black it was
Black   black   black
And the fever was made flesh
And dwelt among us: death-dealing
Fierce and feverish
Laying icy hands   indiscriminate
On all
Father   mother   child
Fair and free
Dark and fettered

And after the leveling
Came the mourning
And the no one
To care   care   care
For the left:
Old with no young   tottering
Young with no old   leaning
Untaught with no hope

And the Shepherd
Lyonnais   alien
Rode weary
From boundary to boundary
Blessing the quick and dead
Scorched and cold
On endless Texas plains
Heart bleeding fire
For a vast and hapless flock
Knowing no care
Of gentle ministering hands
To close the sightless eye
Or soothe the suffering brow

Dubuis the Lyonnais
Left alien home for   home
Searching in Christ's name
Relief in care-full hands
To minister to his people
Scattered and tormented

He found the pristine three
Eager   willing
To set their hands
To plow and not look back
Leading the line
That after came
From France and Deutchsland
Holland   Eire   and Mexico
To join with native hands
To meet Christ's need
Of bringing Him with gentle heart to man

Incarnating
Rooting the word:
In sickness caring
In death   caring
In teaching   caring

Letting Him   live
In bodies made whole
In minds full-formed
In eyes
Closed once on Him in them
To open on Him forever
Bringing men to Christ
And Christ to man
Wording
Incarnating
Rooting
The Gospel God

On Texas soil
From then
To now
To forever

VIAJE (Mexico)

The Road   not for itself
Is strangely infinite   ubiquitous
Making beginnings endings
For you   having been on it or to go
Always there
If only in pieces

Each mile traversed
Is to bring to the next
Till you reach where you get
To stop at your there
And you do
Your beginning ended

Then you don't use the road anymore

Still breaking horizons
Like when you started
Not for itself
Always leading to theres
Each there left
Each beginning ended

Altruistic
The road goes on

"Grave" Yard Fancy

Don't spread plastic flowers

on my grave

just let me be

if you can't bring

blooms

exuding God's creation

and the daisy

 I'd rather—honestly—rot simply

under pure clay

pure weed

just ordinary grass

than dressed atop with tinsel

proclaiming everlastingness

in false color

far from the manufaction underneath
unrelenting and true

B Flight 23, Newark/Dallas/San Antonio, Feb. 11, 1979

I

'Twas the first time I saw from up
The whole earth snowcovered
And after an hour only in crevices
Sunforgotten and etching
Patterns stark into mountains
Reviewing the distant snow
Against airport patterns
Feeling the lonely inevitable sweep
Away from loved ones
Up out into over blue and cloud
I halfheard only the droning welcome captain commercial
Wondering what next flight
Braniff or other
Would once more
Bear me eastwards
To a snow or fall or summer earth
Meeting the lowered wheels

II

Patterns: after Dallas
Looking down at an angle or direct over
It all looks so beguilingly arranged and ordered
As if no mistakes were made:
Highways framing giant browngreen murals monotonous

Collages jewelled of cities   intermittent   discriminating
Lakes occasional and blue-green   shapeless   variegated
Lines are too straight and long
As if some rigid divine human planner defying rivers
Absoluted the expulsion of serpentine ways

Wouldn't you think from here
You could simply
Go where you're going
When you touchdown
And suffer neither baggage of battle
Nor slings and arrows of outrageous traffic
I once saw 24 oiltanks up there
Mausoleums minding the suctioned earthblood
Awaiting another resurrection and final
And I remembered sudden
Minuscule in another land
Other patterns greengreen
And cried they were so distant
While incongruous soft and glorious clouds pillowed
Our motionless motion over a Jordan
Screening new patterns different with silver

After You Left, Feb. 19, 1979

There is everything about you
That I love

In a way you are like God
(creating   in your easy real accepting you)
Because I believe your everything
Knowing your strife for authenticity
After the model we both profess to follow
And hope during days' day upon day
Meandering through the world
To keep the eye attuned   learning
To the meek and humble God
Who is Who is

Divinely narcissistic
Bowing in incarnation
To His creation in you
And making disparity parity
Raising us to Godequal
Through redemption
To unheard of glory

Good Friday: Fasting I

don't draw up or out your face
but rather paint it   plucking
and wear red
a something or other

the single piece of buttered toast
(the rest took two)
looks lonely
you said inside you'd eat it dry

but they don't know   God does   that
you had planned
and went directly to Room 27
to eat the red red apple
from Holy Thursday's oblate providence
offering at 12 last nite
for those   not you
who hadn't time for supper
they don't know either
that every time your tongue
called out for slaking
you ran to drink
despite the voice
"I thirsting" in your ear
am i fasting
and if   for me or them or God
it's hard to say   let's see
do i absolutely   ontologically
totally categorically care about them
would i eat 6 pieces of toast just to show
No
but don't let's dice
about diet and spirit reasons

me: you're used to kidding you
knowing at the core the real thing
the ambiguity   pure   amorphous

then God   there's you
you're always there   aware
beckoning me away from me
prepared to—though not yet—
step kindly in and grace me
with the will   the steady plowing hand

and eyes that don't look back
let's on to lunch and see how goes the soup
i have no cheese in Room 27
but Lord you'd better stay around

Good Friday: Fasting II

after dinner
it's a luxury absolute
whole and entire
to sit here after
and eat my ice
spoonful by spoonful
quietly thinking   watching the stragglers
eke out
and the seconds go up for more
red chunky thick hot tomato soup
and more crackers
others sipping icetea
yes it's a luxury   not Good Friday at all

you don't absolutely have to do anything
you have absolutely nothing to do
except BE
you don't have to move   sneeze maybe
you don't have to go to the bathroom
you can just sit and wait
chuckfully full of your ice icetea and
bowl of hotredchunky soup
and 6 crackers, 3 packages

full you can wait and sit and sit and wait
and write and think and sit and write
and wait in luxury
it's prodigal amid the fast
who can sit like this after
soup and crackers and icetea and ice
and wonder wandering
through the silent chirping
quiet mingling
of the potpourri of Christians gathered
simply   solely   soully   singly
to live exulting in the Good   the News

of Jesus, sun Son, only begotten of God
of David, Mary and the Father
incarnated, incarnating redeeming
who can sit exulting in the sequence
of Christmas springseeding into
Palm's Passion flower
through Autumn's unequivocal denial
through winter's Judas kiss
bleak after the washing
through dereliction stark
and Good of Friday's crosses
into blooming resurrection
summer Sunday's stone rolled back

it's a luxury, Christian, gift, divine
given   the gift itself   Redemption
the sitting fasting on soup thick and red
and crackers   icetea and ice
exulting

PURE NARD

Jesus! pure nard! they were outraged

outrageous out   the guys,   disciples

the ones He'd taught   dis-cip-lined

imagine   that woman approaching

first of all   who let her in   and why in the first place

were they in Simon's house anyway

didn't He know   God   He was such a fool betimes

that leprosy was for sin   He seemed so often not to know the law

they'd have to teach Him later

89

and then anointing   daring slut   to touch Him
did He know who she was   they did   hadn't they
didn't I   well that's my business   but HIM

look at her caressing   smoothing   God!
it looks so sensuous   sinful even   and does she know how!
Lord   You couldn't   He isn't   You're not
He's   actually enjoying it   God!
He doesn't   He couldn't   He musn't know

That smell all over   Pure nard   what a waste
pure positive   prodigality   pure waste

I could have sold it for the poor
Where did she get it   snitched it   very likely
Some rich sunnovabitch   wanted it poured over
his silken slimy body
Jesus! she's using it all   all over all over His feet
she could have bought it herself
something about her   not mean
Jesus!   pure nard!
we'll have to talk to Him about this
in alabaster   pure nard!   Jesus!!!

HOSPITAL NOTEBOOK[35]

Consultant

Before he comes
the staff nurse
after sweeping clear
his path of patient paraphernalia
fusses in
to warn you to expect
preparing

and then he comes
Mr. God, pastor
skilled and humble
the questions on his brow
heading the lineup round the bed
sheep wondering   learning
who follow after
looking for god's nod
to mark this   watch that
listen, hear and   BE
sharp   aware
combining the old skills
with new machinery
primed to root the cause

frustrated by the telltale hiding signs
and puzzled frightened answers
he then outleads his flock
to corridors incisive
perhaps to add   subtract   divide
interpret
and seek the healing answer
then on to other
signs   bodies and patterns
different   though strangely reminiscent
of the first.

Me: human bean

A strange combine of all
I've done and been
done to and been done to
up to now

Afraid of the dark deep
inside of me
wanting to be like TV heroin(e)s
addicted to notoriety and rights
and what I'll do tomorrow
knowing that "but for"
the smile
coming to me from
Christmas first
then you and you and you
the darkest deep will surface
like Paul doing that I dursn't
and not that I durst
into   headlines
and another public statistic
waiting to be used for crime prevention

The Hospital

I've never seen it
only inside waiting
looking at tall walls
green and pale
and through the ancient window
a grey sun lighting the winter tree
leaning over smoke
that steams towards morning moving
clouds sometimes outlined with sunlight
along grey slanted roofs

I'm only in room 4 ground floor
inside waiting   waiting for healing
from the long mustering ministering
parade from 6 to round the clock
coming with qualities of presence
and of presents
with pills and touch and tea
and things
that beckon

The Patient

Doctor   is NOT the body   just
nor hand nor eye nor limb
calling for healing

but deep   deep   deep
the heart pulsating
proclaiming *"patior"*
I suffer   patient-   ly
waiting the skill and eye of you
to answer   deep
the longing within
towards the miraculousity
of wholeness
a new taste on the mouth
and the flight
back to the wholesome day
of trite and homely things
and trivia at home

Decision

after you left
I knew what I must do
over the late and morning hours
reflecting
on my guilt
and panting over the shoulder

at the nemesis
of God's   reckless   unrelenting
pursuit

the thundering call
into the heart
and the moment of the operating   operating
scourging ministers
over mazes of crossed lines
would not be stilled
till fathomless within
I somewhere somehow
slow and beaten
after a thousand and another
yes and no   I will   I won't
drained the threatening chalice and

bowed low

        to all the evolutioning

and agonistic nows
converging towards horizon

For Pop and my Brothers

You big fine Irish

gorgeous gentle men

with your practised casual shrug

and your latest joke

through questioning eyes

shifting on feet

reaching for nicotine

to still the thunder of the heart which

you must under no whatever
circumstances
even and especially flow of spirit(s)
reveal
STOP!
and listen to your crying
in the other shiftless *coggering*[36] voice
living the selfsame lie
and let your making Lord
go on in you
perfectioning the weary wandering job
He started at your birth
and for God's sake
and mine
give Him a hand

Healing

You must wait for me
till time is ripe
and seasons have run
their course
to coreness at the rim
and the moment
we three in one
have planned eternally

to bring to you
in fullness and in love
after the strife
of prep-
and rep-   aration

The Now

we never know
the moment of grace
so must attune to present
with ever listening
and stark naked ear
unafraid
or else the time will pass
and the ripeness
of all the rippling
and infinite consequential spiralings
to the original apex
is now lost eternal
in our deaf hesitancies
and nearly casual refusals

Security

don't take my blanket
the one that holds my soul and soles
together
keeping   out cold   in warm
nursing me on to whole

The WORD

Christ had to die at 33
He couldn't stand
His understanding
of the things He'd made
wilting in layers
of lurking in lines
of loneliness and fear
rejection   grief   denial
and the pain   the pain   the pain
of the haunting hurt
that it might never change

so up He ran to Calvary
after the final night of agony
bloodsweating
to turn at least
at last in His great hour

to one of us and say
"This day thou shalt be with
me in (our) paradise"

Healer

for everything and everyone
a season and a time
I was waiting
hearing the click of
your familiar ICI heels
busy on the long long hall
with wounds and voices
and pain calling out for eyes
the power of them
working through your
delicate soothing woman fingers
knowing
to find the trouble spot

The Patient

sirs and mizzes
3rd person singular
he/ she/ it
is the sum of stress and strife
griefs   fears   imaginings
denials   angers   loves and hates
regrets and human insecurities
that bring him/her/it   to the now
of body broken at some fold
or jointure
waiting your healing hand and heart

that's who
perhaps or what
the patient is

so please you healers
be still with reassurance
and too   don't pass
and unlearning
the faces on your halls
not yet admitted
pinched, pained on duty
proclaiming in their distant eyes
unseeing
stones in the heart
that soon must rupture
into brokenness
any   where

For *Eibhlis* after Hospital Visit

when
EVERYTHING on plates
tasted like
how straw looks
going into the horse's ambling mouth protruding

then I remembered
(relishing your own
concocted marmalade on ryvita
that anathema in diets taste)

YOU
      and after you left
I remember   I remembered
the lilting aroma of your voice
over the hours and ears
Room 4, groundfloor, Hospital I
wafted from the window
of apple-orange and carnations dappled

and now writing
I wonder at me
thinking of you
equal to
marmalade on ryvita
fruits topped with flowers and sun and friendship
and the homely memory
of a country basket chuckfull
hooked on your arm
groomed fine and brown and smart
firmstepping in that young coat
relict of Mam and home
      and I am happy

To Mary C. for Your Hospital Visit

you came to me then
with your little brown being
of hope and eyes and "oh dears"
peeking round my door
creeping in to pick up frazzled
pieces
asking with that smile in your eye
how and who you are at this now
and where begins the pain and ends

offering your Saturday laid waste
in ashes of struggle through
football hordes
on the convoluting train
winding east
towards grey mazes leading long
to nowhere
till you found me

and there
your presents quiet and real and tending
hallmark of you
and salved with your utmost presence tendered
and you fragile
yet strangely strong
bearing certainly to me
across the miles and sea and hours
the whole brewed posse of incarnating lines
from yellow fever days and Texas prairies
to the now of the voice on the line
ministering

and then, I say
you melted out again
into grey streets and strange
to find me
somewhere somehow
hidden in some cluttered huxter's
a nail scissors

The Pain

as it really is in itself
at the heart of the matter
harrowing
is just like itself
not anything else
not like cold on the nose in snow
nor wet, on legs in rain

stark tollpiece heralding death and
other world
sinister   waiting
creeping   stealthily
nagging   inevitable
or lurching sudden
clutching
through bone or marrow
or indefinably

through joints somewhere
going nowhere special
but there   just there
real as a boil on the cheek burning
or a splinter beating a little finger
anywhere
into a rhythmic tattoo
throbbing places afire in your leg
you never noticed before
when they were whole
quiet   working and cool

Funerals in Ireland

the neighbors never die at the right time
their funerals and rosaries
intrude on your plans to go fishing
or shopping or mitching[37]
you shuffle off trussed up in a hurry
to Jack Mac's last Mass
grumbling inside wishing he'd waited
till next week or even tomorrow

and there you are *mise en scène*[38]
in face suitable lined up condoling
clutching vague hands one by one
muttering uncomfortable phrases
wondering who's who

of brothers and sisters heard mentioned
now and again
last seen drunk at a wedding

thrusting your Mass card
duly signed by his reverence hovering
into a lap   convulsed
or furtively casting an eye around
self-conscious
you slide it onto the coffin

and then deep-breathing relieved
at another duty done diligent
you step on out to a casual day
of your affairs
thinking it's the same with visitors
they come when you're going out
or with a foot in the bath
and saying inside without noticing
I wonder if it'll all be the same when I go

Legs: Renewed

the legs   are all   nearly   bare now
loose in wind and sun and dust
toes wriggling free and open
variously sandaled in rainbow
and colors subdued emerging

remembering the long years
chemised to knees
of swathings tri-deep

105

of black-green cotton enclosing
and full underskirts
caverned with pockets convoluting and heavy
topped voluminously and neat
with pleats symmetrical and serge
the legs exult
golden from sun and shaved

I remember novitiate evenings peering
a hard wood darning egg
overmarked with my number VI 740
under hours of interminable holes
patterning once more criss-cross
the heel and toe
black on green-black cotton

Surveying legs again
I note the years of service
registered in veins blue-purple
outreaching

now new sunburned and browned

somewhere on some sand or pool or beach
or raised deck-chaired and tired
on cloistered porch
reaching for gift of sun

and silently I muse
from whence we came
there are no black stockings
on any legs today

You, CCVI[39], my own

You, CCVI, my own
you, answering my call
from the long years
across eachday moments
of the now
over hills and seas
alien to alien
with the heart unsure
yet opened in *suscipe*
receiving
my sacrament of the present
pressing forward
carried   reassured
in my caress   jealous and divine
greeting you   smiling
in the once more
fiat of your tired and open heart
looking for wholeness
in my converging now
you, my own
come. . . .

Track Laps, before seven

the three blue-towards-lavender wild flowers
dainty   enduring
by the just two winedrops drooping
catch my eye each lap
as I round the ellipse

them passed, I go on
waiting in hope
for the joy and rest of the color of them
again after the hard and grey and monotone
of the dull macadam
meeting the even steps
of my challenged soles
and the changing panorama
of morning grass and net wire
under skies grey-blue and brightening
converging with treetops and power lines
and the silhouette of an eclectic condo

and my body cutting through
the thick morning heavy air
osmosing out
the wonderfully healthy sweat
that crawls down
the base of my skull and backbone tickling

the mockers at intervals
concerting with a lone last cricket echoic
and the background buzz
of traffic on 410 east orchestrate
the panting voices
of joggers stepping rhythmically by
shaking contours and layers even in steady unison

happily wet all over I pant out my sixth lap
and mounting the steps over the riverbed

dry and vistaing from up   an infant forest
I think of oranges and coffee
and the forbidden aroma
of bacon   crisp and inviting

ELEGY: Chapter[40] Planning

I don't think we planned

that

Pat Kelley

Montsy Patino

Anne Smiley

Or Magdalena Rojo

Would not be here for Chapter '90

To say nothing of the twin exodus of the Healions

Our best laid plans

Like those of mice

Gang aft awry

His ways not ours

I LIKE YOU MY CONGREGATION BECAUSE

You took me in all green and young and ignorant and eager 40 years ago

I feel one with you, many and varied, long short, fat thin, silent talkative, faraway near, prayerful, tired, energetic, always with eyes on the holy goal and wanting to be there

You led me through times thick and thin:

the all-knowing teens

the wondering twenties

the questioning thirties

the questing forties

the now still wondering and wandering fifties

You let me go to Pop to help him die

You sent me to college, courses, talks, workshops, retreats, and challenged me in the mission here, there and yonder

You taught me how to pray

I saw, still see, prayer, kindness and the two commandments personified

Sister Florence was such a practical lady interviewing Angelica, Olivia and me

way back there in Mother Mary John's niece's parlor

Miss May O'Sullivan, North Circular Road, Dublin

And let us come to Dunmore

Sister Mary Lucy took her sickness and death so gracefully

Mike, Clarencia, Gertrude and others write to me way down here in Huancané

Mary Pep is still going strong at what, nearly 90?

I learned Spanish before I died

I'm going to Chapter '90, first time delegate

We don't have to carry broken dishes around anymore or ask for a penance

We are sisters of the Word

We all wash dishes still and like our house clean
We are good to the poor
We take care of our "treasurers" at 4707

The Bishop Feels

He said in the Assembly
"It grieves me that we don't communicate"
And I answered out loud
"I'm glad that the Bishop
is saying 'it grieves me'
Because to say that out loud in Assembly
Means the heart is talking
Not the head.

And maybe, who knows, perhaps
There will be communication
Which has already begun now really

With the Bishop telling us "It grieves me."

The Morgue

The eight corpses were laid out on the floor
If you looked closely
You'd see where the bullet entered.
Leopoldo's brains were pouring over his neck.
Fermín's[41] half open eye surprised, seemed to say,
"What did you do to my other eye?"

I took out my oil of the sick
And blessed them one by one,
Praying harder over the two Senderistas[42]
Wondering how many they felled
Before they fell.

In a corner thrown aside
I saw two black pasamontañas.[43]
Did they hide their faces
To not see blood spurting live and red
From heads?

Gettysburg Addressed

NOT WORDS

NOT RITE NOR RIGHT

Not power

Can I or you or both or all or many
Conceive
To consecrate
This hallowed shrine

Whose holy wholeness
Calls pilgrim feet to worship
   now and ever
For blood poured down profuse and red
By countless
Knowing or not knowing (as they did)
Their own awareness of the fittingness
That one should die for all

But let devotion so measure full
In me and thee endure
To that their cause and ours
(One nation under God
Birthing free and equal
By, for and of the people governed
Not to ever perish)
That to dedicate this their ground
Be not just proper fitting noble resolute
But brave and power full and holy

Gift

The Blessed Mother winked at me last night in my dream
and when suddenly I realized what she'd done
and was afraid she hadn't

(because   I really shouldn't go into this now
since it's breaking up what I'm telling you about the gift
so that's why it's in parentheses   you can come back to it later
because, as I was saying
I'm a bigger sinner   inner   than ever Paul or Augustine
always reneging
and never remembering her either
and I've no mother still alive to pray for me

and work miracles till I die
or get totally converted
and be made bishop
nor a horse to be struck blind down off of
and I can't ride anyhow
and if ever you want to ask me about it you can
the sinning I mean
and I might tell you)

I asked her again in the blink of an eye
even before she had the wink finished
to give me another sign
to do something else
and you know what
she did
she let the loveliest of a long smile
ripple over her whole teenage face
in a pinkness and flushness and youngness   lush
you'd never believe
that just wouldn't go away even when my dream was over
and I was waking up remembering
I had to tell her
I did it again Ma, I God-oofed bad
I did   Will you tell Him?

Prose Poem

This is a story of two coyotes and a black cat named Bright
Eyes emerging out of kittenhood. The two coyotes were lean.
The she was speckled in the distance. She moved with a purpose.
She did not sense me. I kept watching. Then she was gone around
the trees.

Bright Eyes lapped the milk on the porch warily. With
caution she moved in front of me toward the big house, stopping
every few steps to look back, eyes wide, wild in terror,
questioning. She'd felt the presence. We went up to the house.
She never stopped looking back, her eyes brighter, bluer and wider
each time. She stayed near me.

The next time the two coyotes were there. I was in the
chapel at the window. I saw movement over by the water hole.
Something rose up, stretched and nosed around. I only knew it
was the second coyote, the he, when the she rose up out of the
grass and the two of them rounded the water hole and moved off
into the trees where she had gone before. The cows, transfixed,
watched, careful, their heads turning to follow the movement of the
two coyotes. The calf seemed unaware. Bright eyes wasn't there.
The last time I saw them, they emerged from the water hole again,
took a path away from the motionless cows, and disappeared
around the corner of the house. I knew the speckled one was the
she because I had seen her teats dragged and worn the first time.
Next day I went away from that place. This happened in Arkansas
in a country area off Highway 22 where I had gone for six days of
silence and retreat.

Lebh Shomea:[44] Silence 'N' Solitude

In the silence
There's only the rustling
Of the breeze 'n' trees
Branches swaying, praying
Dancing ballerinas
Sweeping across the air
The winds directing
Their paths
In sound and motion
Figures and turns
Suddenly stopped
Or slowly changing rhythm
To a gradual quiescence
Until once more
The music starts
While no bird sings.

Life After Life

When I die

My pilgrimage will be over

My time will have stretched

Into eternity

And I will see with God

The all of eternity

Which did not begin

Which will not end

When I die

Breakfasts

The cows, browns and blacks, two white-faced
And a sprinkling of piebald here and there
All heifers, all pregnant, (the sisters told me)
The bull, black and vigilant
Waiting, watching as I passed tentative

From my hermitage picture window, I watch
In twos, close together, heads down
In the morning grass mixed patches
Of dewy green and hay new mowed
The silence and sound of biting and munching
Intent and happy

I note a stretched occasional headflick
Loose leaves of grass flying from busy mouth
To chase the swarm of hungry flies
Ensconced on flank, tenacious
Escaping the industry of swinging tails
Tireless, bent on moving them
Meanwhile some cheeky birdlets
Martins   swallows   sparrows   finches?
Pounce down in under bovine heads
One playfully brushing the front thigh
Of the lead cow   big and important
Scooping up breakfast enroute
While she   powerful   pays no attention
But stays in contemplative devotion
To the morning ritual   even when
Most daring   another hops close
Around her mouth garnering

Breakfast on "critters" unearthed
Disturbed by bovine feeders
Now faced with sudden end

I remember once in Zambia
My first glimpse of elephant
Monumental   aware   knowing his power
Breakfasting alone on roots
The burgeoning tree he'd just laid low
In Kafue National Park

I drain the mug of my own ritual coffee
Wandering and wondering
About the myriad creatures great and small
Around   down under   in   on earth   sky and sea
Breakfasting.

Requiem: Final Dressings

For my sister, Sister Olivia, C.C.V.I.
April 2003

When I'm dead
Somebody else will dress me
In my grave clothes
There will be no shoes
But they will put on my glasses
So I will look like myself maybe
And the mourners will pass looking down
Perhaps they'll say
You'd think she was sleeping
Look at her skin

I remember when I was young
The Archbishop's wake
I found him alone at the Angelus Funeral Home
And I wondered why they had left on his glasses
And like that
As if they were not on him
But suspended above his nose in the air
And why he was alone
And where were all the people and the priests?

And then I left him alone too

And now I'm remembering our jubilee practice last year
When I went up to the main altar
And saw the coffin at the Blessed Mother's side
I said who's that
She looks so young
It was Clare Eileen
With Olivia sick
I hadn't known she'd died
She was eighty-something
Maybe near ninety
Going to meet our God
With a youthful blush
Her face gone back years
Some other body dressed her too
And the Archbishop
That's just the way it is when we go
Somebody dresses us
Just like they did when we came

When Olivia died
Agnes and Anne asked me for her clothes
We need dress, slip, and panties.
Shoes? I asked,
No, no shoes, they said.
I thought, Olivia's feet will be cold.

I read once that Trappists are buried

in their habits   no coffin.
In Peru Fr. Conrado had requested
he be buried in his poncho, no coffin either
just like the Andean people he left home to serve.

Lent: Calvary

LORD
What was worst
On that hill?
Don't tell me
I know   I was there

And the best?
I think I know:
When that smiling thief
Outrageous to the end
Looked up at You and said
"Lord, remember me. . . . "

And You, smiling too   replied
"This day. . . ."
Isn't that why You came
Messiah, Jesus, Savior, Lord?

Haiku for Desert Mothers

Ah Amas, did sand
(Where was there any water?)
Stick between your toes?

Aging and Thinking

Nobody ever told me about all the things
That happen to you when you are 83 or on the way

When I was 21 I thought my friend who was 33
Was very old

When I was 68 a little boy who thought
I was very very old guessed my age
At about a hundred

And now that I am seriously on the way
To that 100 I don't want to tell anyone
About those happenings I mentioned above
It might discourage them

I remember once starting a poem with
If I were God . . . I went on to say
I'd sweep everything under the carpet
Permanently and let everyone in

And –think about this—
Since I am made in His image
I expect He does that too

Today I read that St. Padre Pio said
"Whatever wrong you might do

Your guardian angel would never leave you
Pray, hope and don't worry, worry is useless
God is merciful and will hear your prayer."

Before Bed

I was going to do something
Now I don't know what it was
And now I still don't know
What it was

I'm looking around me
At the book on the nightstand
And feeling the cool
Of the fan I changed
To third speed
The slowest of three
I still don't know what it was

I was going to do

What would *Hafiz* [45] do in a case like this
He'd laugh and laugh and laugh
And then turn out the light
And say his prayers
Faithful, sacrilegious, like himself.

The Neighbor: 2 Haikus

Someone at the door
I'm busy please go away
Importunance   GOD !!!

Neighbor at the door
Come in the door is open
Importunate God   !!!

The Tax Collector   (*Luke 19:1-10*)

What will I do   I want to see Him

The crowd is so big   they won't let me near

When they see who I am

They said He's different, not like the others

There's a tree up there   a sycamore

I'll run and climb it   yes I can see Him from here

He's coming this way   and looking up

He sees me   O God   He's calling me

He wants to come to my house   to eat   my God

I'll kill the calf   I'll tell Him   about my sins   my money

That I'll give to the poor   and pay back the ones I cheated

Give them more   four times more   I'll ask Him what else

He'll know

He's here   O my God   come in Lord   sit down   over here

I'll get water for Your feet   let me soak them for you

We'll eat and drink and sing and laugh together

O God I don't deserve this   me Zachaeus   the tax collector

O Jesus   thank You   thank You   thank You O my God

God Online

Hasta cuándo[16] (Reader, your name comes here)
Will you keep on not believing
When I whisper I love you;
When I tell you I never leave,
Since before you were in the womb?
That I am the voice you hear in the silence
Saying, "yes, do"   or   "no, run the other way."
Just ask me.   I'm here,
Waiting for you.   Where are you?

Awards Ceremony:
Perspective: 1916-1966

Address by Mr. George J. Colley, T.D., Minister for Education, on the occasion of his presenting at Iveagh House, Dublin on Monday, 23 May 1966 at 3:00 p.m., prizes for literature, music and art offered by the 1916 Golden Jubilee Commemoration Committee.

Dear Friends,

Few duties have given me more pleasure than this one. I say this because I am certain that poetry, music and art, more than anything else other than the events of the Rising itself, would appeal to the leaders of the Rising, as their mark of honor.

Amongst those executed at that time, without looking beyond the sixteen, were poets (many of them), dramatists, artists, musicians and novelists. I doubt if there was ever a similar uprising in which artists generally played a greater part. You have therefore reason to be proud that God has granted you the privilege not only to follow their footsteps but also to celebrate their memory.

If ever a Rising was cradled in art, it was that of Easter, 1916. As Pearse pointed out, the revolutionaries went to school in the halls of the Gaelic League, which, in the hands of Pearse himself, to go no further with names, was a creative literary movement. In the English language one of its sources was the "Celtic Twilight" literature, of which Yeats was the greatest exponent.

In other creative fields also there was, I think, an effort to escape from the hideous art forms (Douglas Hyde's adjective for them) which were often the manner of the time, a product, as Hyde believed, of the slave mentality that went with an anglicized Ireland.

Generally, indeed, the period of which the Rising was the culmination, as well as showing forth the promise of great political and social changes, was throbbing with intellectual and cultural activity. To the rising generation of those days and to some who were older but still glimpsed the vision splendid, it must almost have seemed as if the horsemen had ridden forth at last from Aileach. (Place in Northern Ireland where ancient heroes lived. The building was called a ring fort because of its circular structure.)

It was natural, therefore, that the burgeoning of that second spring should quickly evoke tribute from many of our artists. They were responding to what their instinct told them was a happening of profound significance. The feeling that they then placed on record was still to convey much of the surge and excitement, the pride and the strength of spirit which would otherwise have been beyond recapture for most of us by the time we had reached the age of understanding.

In the same way if we ourselves and posterity are to understand better our own feelings, fifty years after, about that most extraordinary week in our near two thousand years of history, our attitude too can best be caught, not through the intellect alone, but through the intellect and the senses combined. In other words, while no doubt we may safely leave to our historians the describing of our political, social and economic circumstances, the best interpreter of feeling is the creative artist.

For these reasons the cultural competitions were an admirable concept on the part of the Commemoration Committee, and it is no less fitting that today's function, the presentation of the awards in these competitions, should crown, as it were, the proceedings of the commemoration.

The list of prizewinners contains a number of names already familiar to us in the field of writing, drama, sculpture and journalism. These names are a guarantee of standard, but I feel sure that the works of those whose names we have not heard before are also of high quality. Indeed, while it would be invidious of me to select individuals for mention here, there are two of these hitherto "unknown soldiers" in particular whom I think you will allow me to except from the rule, An Siúr Maíre Fiontan and Sister Mary Rita Prendergast, winners of the Irish and English poetry competitions respectively.

In their two remarkable poems, each well worthy of a place in a 1916 anthology, we see, if I have read them aright, the two sides of a medal. One shows in the finest traditional mode the "strange, heroic questioning of fate" that was the Rising. The staccato idiom and ironic-seeming matter-of-factness of the other show it as seen looking backward from 1966.

One often wonders how such an episode is really seen by the artist. One wonders, for instance, if he feels it simply as an individual or is the unconscious interpreter of something deep down in the consciousness of his community. I suppose that is your own secret, if indeed even you yourselves are fully aware of how you come to compose a poem or a painting or a sculpture or a sonata.

One could go on philosophizing forever on such mysteries and end as far as ever from the core of the matter—but it is a fact that the first song of note to express popular feeling in the wake of the executions, namely, "Who fears to speak of Easter Week?" was also written by a nun.

Whether that is of special significance I leave to the experts, but at any rate it is a very pleasant duty for me to congratulate an Siúr Maíre Fiontan and Sister Mary Rita; and it is no less pleasant a duty to congratulate all of you. *Mo ghoirm sibh! Go mairidh sibh bhur saothar. (Well done! May you live to enjoy your achievement.)*

Acknowledgements

THANKS first to You, my God, for creating me, for the parents You chose for me and the family we became.

For the Presentation Sisters, who in kindergarten through secondary school, opened to me the joy of reading, writing, arithmetic, and the penny catechism. A very special thanks to the teacher who encouraged me to write my very first poem! That was truly the beginning of this present effort.

I thank God for my vocation to the Sisters of Charity of the Incarnate Word and for my Congregation who received me, taught me how to pray and become a Sister, educated me and allowed me to minister to God's people on various missions.

I am grateful to my volunteer helpers who, since January 2013, have been encouraging me in many ways to bring this book to life. In 2000, Ruth Fowler, Incarnate Word College alumna, teacher, administrator, homemaker and friend, sent me a disc with all my poems on it as well as a hard copy of the poems, telling me it was time to publish them. I was touched and grateful but not ready.

Then, in 2013, Sister Margaret Patrice, my first English teacher at Incarnate Word College, reminded me in no uncertain terms that "time was flying and that I should publish my poems before...." When she stopped there, I added: "I die?" She replied: "Yes." This time the work began.

Out of the blue came Sister Louise Delisi, ready and willing with her computer skills to do the groundwork which was heavy, non-stop and not always clear. Sister Margaret Patrice had warned us early on that we would have to read, revise, and check many times before we would be ready for the printer. Thank you, Sisters Margaret and Louise--there is no way I could have done it without you. And thanks to you, all my Sisters, who by your presence and prayer, have encouraged me along the way.

Special thanks to Ed Jackson of Cathedral Church Supplies who informed and reassured us about the use of Millet's painting "The Gleaners", prepared a sample cover and answered our questions about details of publishing. Thanks to our Congregational Archivist, Donna Guerra, for gracious and prompt research on historical facts, names and dates, and computer skills and mysteries which Sister Louise deeply appreciated. Thanks also to Matthew Reyna, Director of Volunteers at the Village at Incarnate Word, who came for computer fixes at crises moments.

Much gratitude to Tom Burke, a quiet Irish scholar, teacher and guru from Cloonfad, County Roscommon, Ireland, for his translation from the Irish.

To all others who supported me with words of encouragement and prayer I offer a very grateful "Thank you!" and a prayer that God bless all of you all your days and may He hold you in the palm of His hand.

Sister Rita Prendergast, C.C.V.I.

Notes

1.Let it be done.

2. The three poems following are related to the "Irish Question" which made Ireland a part of the World War II picture. "Odyssey '66" is concerned with guerilla war days in Ireland in the 1920's and the response of the Irish conscience. "Perspective" looks back at the 1916 Rebellion from a 50-year stance, reminiscing on how it came about and what it cost in lives, living, and finances. "Perspective" was the winning poem in the English language section of the 1916 Golden Jubilee Commemoration Competition. (See p. 125 for awards ceremony account.) "Sonnet for Pearse" eulogizes the schoolteacher-poet, visionary and dreamer, Padraig Pearse, who was among the group of leaders who planned a rebellion that faced impossible odds.

3. This poem is written in stream-of-consciousness form. The speaker in the poem lets his mind run where it will, not always in a logical direction, as in a dream, not explicable.

4. Royal Irish Constabulary, the English police system in Ireland; in the mind of the Irish, the enemy.

5. But.

6. Headquarters.

7. Reference to an Irish boat tragedy in which many people died. The Irish reference *ag síleadh súl* (eyes dripping tears) and

the Latin from Virgil, *Hic sunt lacrymae rerum*, (The Tears of Things), both refer to the sadness of the human struggle in general, and in this case, the struggle for Irish Independence.

8. An Irish derogatory, disparaging word for an Englishman who was seen as a colonizer and enemy.

9. Officer in Command.

10. Auxiliaries: another police group who seemingly were in charge of curfew. The Black and Tans (named for colors they wore) were untrained, armed terrorist groups sent from England to control the Irish rebels. They rode around in lorries (trucks) making sudden appearances at will. It was said they were prisoners from English jails released to form these groups. My mother remembered them coming to her home, bursting in and taking the food, including freshly baked bread and new-laid eggs. On the way out they shot a cow.

11. See footnote #2

12. Dublin must be destroyed.

13. Furious indignation.

14. Law of the Czar.

15. Popular British singer, winner of national Eurovision Song Contest with "Puppet on a String."

16. Our world.

17. German: *Sturm und Drang*: Storm and Stress

18. Plentiful, flowing; LSD: initials for Irish currency; drug.

19. Calphurnius and Conchessa: St. Patrick's parents.

20. Town in which St. Patrick's parents lived.

21. St. Patrick's pre-Christian name.

22. Hill in Co. Meath where Druids and later Christians held religious ceremonies.

23. There is no accounting for tastes.

24. (And you, too   what a pity   and you!)

25. Virgil: "Here are the tears of things."

26. Flowing tears.

27. You cannot give what you haven't got.

28. As is necessary.

29. Race course.

30. Midden: a mound or deposit containing shells, animal bone, and other refuse that indicate the site of a human settlement.

31. Here lies.

32. These are the tears of things.

33. I for sure can't do it.

34. Oblates of Mary Immaculate retreat house in San Antonio, Texas.

35. "Hospital Notebook" consists of the sixteen poems that follow which were written during a time of personal illness.

36. From the Irish, *cogar*: to whisper.

37. Irish used to describe children skipping school; also adult night visits of neighbors, unannounced and generally overstaying welcome.

38. French term used in staging drama: right in place.

39. Initials for the Latin form of The Congregation of the Sisters of Charity of the Incarnate Word.

40. Congregational planning meeting.

41. Leopoldo and Fermin were indigenous men who helped our Congregational missionaries in Peru during the time of the Shining Path Terrorists.

42. Shining Path, a terrorist group in Peru.

43. Black woolen masks which have slits for the eyes.

44. Retreat House in Sarita, Texas.

45. Persian poet, 14th century.

46. How long.